Sunday Thoughts

Sunday Thoughts

A Year of Finding God

MARKIE DOCZI

Foreword by VAL RAHAMUT

RESOURCE *Publications* · Eugene, Oregon

SUNDAY THOUGHTS
A Year of Finding God

Resource Publications
An Imprint of Wipf and Stock Publishers
199 W. 8th Ave., Suite 3
Eugene, OR 97401

www.wipfandstock.com

PAPERBACK ISBN: 979-8-3852-1429-7
HARDCOVER ISBN: 979-8-3852-1430-3
EBOOK ISBN: 979-8-3852-1431-0

To John and Linda, who got us back to church.

"All scripture is given by inspiration of God, and is profitable for doctrine, for reproof, for correction, for instruction in righteousness" (2 Timothy 3:16, KJV).

Contents

CONTENTS

Foreword

MARKIE DOCZI HAS A unique way of taking a scripture and turning it into food for thought for this day and time. She offers practical insights on how to live a Christian life, and ways to apply them during one's personal circumstances. She describes in plain language aspects of daily life events, asks questions, and then gives answers that glorify God and the path He has directed for each person.

Every devotion will help to equip and teach you to rely on the Holy Spirit for every aspect of your life as He grows your faith. This is an anointed book with many great life lessons that we can use to fulfill our destiny in the Kingdom of God. I highly recommend this book, as it will contribute to your spiritual growth and your personal time spent with Him.

Val Rahamut, BSN, RN, ThA, ThB
President and Co-founder of
World Christian Outreach Ministries

Introduction

HI, I'M MARKIE. THANK you for picking up my book! *Sunday Thoughts* began as a simple idea (or a thought, as it were). After being driven away from social media for a couple of years due to all of the discouraging content, I finally decided to go back; only, instead of letting the negativity get me down, I would share positive scriptural thoughts each week to lift others up. In a matter of weeks, those simple "thoughts" had blossomed into full-blown devotions—and now, a book!

We all have questions, and daily struggles in this life. And while I certainly don't pretend to have all the answers, in these pages I address some of those issues, such as negativity and unforgiveness. I also explore some topics which are viewed differently amongst the Christian denominations, like baptism and luck.

Sunday Thoughts is written from a Christian perspective and reinforced with Scripture. I offer my opinions, and Biblical references as to why I feel that way. I encourage you, dear reader, to study the referenced verses provided and come to your own conclusions! God has blessed my humble endeavor, and may He bless you in yours.

Sunday Thought:
In the Beginning

In the beginning, man met his end
But now thanks to Jesus, the Lord and the Lamb,
We die to begin life again.

Where better to begin than the beginning? There are two prominent beliefs regarding how all life came into being: creation and evolution. As this is an expansive topic, I will simply touch on some of the key contrasting points.

I hope this brief study will strengthen the beliefs of new Christians; and, if you are on the fence as to which explanation you believe, I hope it will motivate you to continue investigating for yourself!

The very first chapter of the Bible tells us how God created the heavens and earth.[1] We are told that this creation took six days, and on the seventh day, he rested:

"And on the seventh day God ended his work which he had made; and he rested on the seventh day from all his work which he had made" (Genesis 2:2, KJV).

1. Genesis 1

To this day, our calendars mark a seven day week; and Sundays have always been set aside, both for God and for rest.

The theory of evolution was introduced two hundred years ago, whereas the belief in creation has been around since the beginning of time—but how long ago was that?

Evolutionists claim that the earth is 4.5 billion years old. We Christians believe, in accordance with the timeline of the Bible, that the earth is around 6,000 years old.

To this day, our years are measured in terms of B.C. (Before Christ) and A.D. (Anno Domino, which translates to 'in the year of our Lord').

What about those inexplicable things that have held us in awe for generations, like the advanced sunken cities we've discovered, or the great pyramids? Where the theory of evolution suggests that we descended through apes and cave men, God's Word tells us that mankind was created an intelligent being.

Let's use the human body as an example. Laid end to end, an adult's blood vessels would encircle the earth four times. Roughly two-thirds of the human body is composed of water (very similar to the composition of the earth). We have immune systems, natural filters, and brains with amazing capabilities. It seems plain to me that we were designed.

"And the Lord God formed man of the dust of the ground, and breathed into his nostrils the breath of life; and man became a living being" (Genesis 2:7, NKJV).

There is also the important topic of the Great Flood. In Genesis chapter six, God told Noah that He would destroy the earth;[2] and in chapter seven, He did so.

2. Genesis 6:13

"And after the seven days the flood waters came on the earth. And rain fell on the earth forty days and forty nights" (Genesis 7:10,12, NIV).

Evolutionists have long claimed that multiple layers of earth take millions of years to form; yet there is a type of fossil called polystrate, which can be found in various locations around the globe. These fossils are upright trees (some upside down) that are buried by many layers of earth. Millennia-long processes cannot account for this anomaly—but a catastrophic flood can.

Scientists also learned, in the aftermath of the 1980 eruption of Mount St. Helens, that multiple layers of earth can form within a brief span of time.

Darwin defined evolution as "descent with modification." Creationists believe that after the Great Flood, there was speciation within kinds—but not evolution of one kind into another. Life cannot come from non-life.

Most scholars, including many non-Christians, agree that there is sufficient evidence of a catastrophic global flood (such as the marine fossils found on Mt. Everest, the highest point on the earth). They also concur that Jesus of Nazareth lived, and that he was crucified on the cross. Since these events have been historically and scientifically proven as fact, isn't Jesus—and his Good News[3]—worth looking into?

"By the word of the Lord the heavens were made, and by the breath of his mouth all their host" (Psalm 33:6, ESV).

3. 1 Corinthians 15:3-4

At the end of the day, it requires more faith to believe in evolution than it does to believe in God. Let's express some gratitude for God's beautiful creation.

Dear God, thank you for another day in your beautiful creation. Please help me to share your truth with others that they may see your glory, both in themselves and throughout nature.

Your Thoughts . . .

_____

_____

_____

_____

_____

_____

_____

_____

_____

_____

_____

_____

_____

_____

_____

_____

_____

_____

_____

_____

_____

_____

_____

Sunday Thought:

The Rainbow

A prism of color reminds of a promise
Made long ago from on High
Suspended in place whence the promise came,
That stroke of a moment for only as long
Again draws to heaven our eye.

Where did the rainbow come from? And what does it mean? We read about the first rainbow in Genesis, after God destroyed the world with the Great Flood:

"I set my rainbow in the cloud, and it shall be for the sign of the covenant between me and the earth. And I will remember my covenant which is between me and you and every living creature of all flesh; the waters shall never again become a flood to destroy the flesh" (Genesis 9:13,15, NKJV).

The rainbow serves as a reminder not only to us, but to God, of his promise to never again destroy the earth by flood waters. Interestingly, this beautiful sign only appears during or after a rain—that same element which destroyed the earth so long ago. What a humbling reminder.

Heavenly Father, I thank you for your promise and its beautiful symbol. Help me to lean on you during the hard times so that I come out stronger on the other side, just as the rainbow shines through after a storm.

Your Thoughts . . .

_____

_____

_____

_____

_____

_____

_____

_____

_____

_____

_____

_____

_____

_____

_____

_____

_____

_____

_____

_____

Sunday Thought:

The Meaning of Life

Let us consider Solomon, the wisest in the land
As we begin to contemplate our purpose,
and your plan.

HAVE YOU EVER FOUND yourself wondering, what's the point of it all? The ups and downs, the unstoppable march of time—all leading to inevitable death.

At a glance, it paints a pretty bleak picture. But let's explore the big question that most of us have asked at some point: What is the meaning of life?

This is a question than man has been asking himself since Biblical times. King Solomon was the wealthiest and wisest man of the land; yet, when he considered life apart from God, it was empty:

"Meaningless! . . . Utterly meaningless! . . . Everything is meaningless" (Ecclesiastes 1:2, NIV).

"There is no remembrance of former things, nor will there be any remembrance of things that are to come by those who will come after" (Ecclesiastes 1:11, NKJV).

I love that last verse, and advise you to read it again. No matter what legacies we leave behind, they *will* be forgotten eventually. But when our names are written in the book of life, that endures forever.

If you are at a low point in your life and you don't know Jesus, know that there *is* a point to it all. Get to know your Savior, and you'll understand.

"The end of the matter; all has been heard. Fear God and keep His commandments, for this is the whole duty of man" (Ecclesiastes 12:13, ESV).

If you are reading this and are already a Christian, but struggling to the point of asking yourself this question, then I hope these words have reminded and encouraged you! Never forget the powerful words of Paul when he wrote to the Philippians:

"I can do all things through Christ who strengthens me" (Philippians 4:13, NKJV).

Dear God, I am grateful for the life you've given me. Forgive me when I'm down on myself and doubting. Remind me that you have a plan for my life.

Your Thoughts . . .

_____

_____

_____

_____

_____

_____

_____

_____

_____

_____

_____

_____

_____

_____

_____

_____

_____

_____

_____

_____

_____

_____

_____

_____

_____

_____

_____

Sunday Thought:
Why Go to Church?

We draw our strength in fellowship
Through sharing of God's power
To rout the roaring lion
Seeking whom he may devour.

I BELIEVE THAT GOING to church is imperative for Christians. This is not to say that you can't have a relationship with God without attending services—after all, the church is the people, not the building—but in order to stay strong against the opposition of the world and maintain that strength, there is much to be gained in fellowship with one another!

Christians are just people, like everyone else, facing the same difficulties and aggravations throughout the week. We worry about money, get impatient with our kids, argue with our spouses . . . the list goes on.

The *difference* is, we all have God in common. We strive to live a godly life in an ungodly world. So when we get together, it's a time of refreshing fellowship where we can celebrate the One we have in common, and lift each other up. The Bible tells us to encourage one another, and not give up meeting together:

"And let us consider one another in order to stir up love and good works, not forsaking the assembling of ourselves together . . ." (Hebrews 10:24,25, NKJV).

"For where two or three are gathered in my name, there am I among them" (Matthew 18:20, ESV).

If you are searching for God, beginning your Christian journey, or feeling alone in it, go to church! Visit different congregations. I always tell people that my husband and I were "church shopping" when we landed at Ash Street Church, our home congregation. The right church will welcome you with open arms, show you God's love, and make you want to go back.

Lord, I am thankful to be made in your image. Thank you for your church, where I can meet other Christians, fellowship, and be uplifted. Guide me to where you would have me go, Lord, and help me to be an instrument of encouragement to those around me, that your love might shine through.

Your Thoughts . . .

_____

_____

_____

_____

_____

_____

_____

_____

_____

_____

_____

_____

_____

_____

_____

_____

_____

_____

_____

_____

_____

_____

_____

_____

_____

_____

_____

_____

_____

Sunday Thought:
Something In the Water

The invitation is open,
As are the arms of the Father
Wade in today, you need not wait
For the stirring of the water.

At the beginning of 2023, our pastor felt that God was telling him it was to be a year of revival. Sure enough, our small congregation steadily grew throughout the year—and that Fall, we had five baptisms within eight days!

There must be something in the water, right?

Physical baptism is symbolic of the death, burial, and resurrection of Christ. It is a public profession of faith, and, if you haven't already, acceptance of God's gift of salvation. (Here you die to your sins.) You are then buried (plunged beneath the water), and resurrected as a new person (brought up from the water).

Once you have attained salvation, the Holy Spirit comes to live within you. The Spirit himself is a tremendous gift, as he intercedes with God for us,[4] and grants us spiritual discernment when we study the Word.

We are exhorted to be baptized, both spiritually and physically. When John the Baptist spoke of the coming of the Christ, he said:

"I indeed baptized you with water, but He will baptize you with the Holy Spirit" (Mark 1:8, NKJV).

"'And now why are you waiting? Arise and be baptized, and wash away your sins, calling on the name of the Lord'" (Acts 22:16, NKJV).

If you are waiting to get baptized until you kick a bad habit or improve yourself in some way, stop waiting. We will never be worthy of the gift of salvation, which is why we are saved by *grace*. We are all imperfect humans, and will inevitably make mistakes, baptized or not.

"For by grace you have been saved through faith, and that not of yourselves; it is the gift of God, not of works, lest anyone should boast" (Ephesians 2:8–9, NKJV).

When Jesus died on the cross he said, "It is finished." This ended the tradition of animal sacrifices for the forgiveness of sins. His sacrifice forgave all past, present, and future sins of the world. Though this is hard to comprehend, we must remember that when Jesus died, all of today's sins were yet future.

So don't wait to be "good enough."

4. Romans 8:26

God, I thank you for your grace, by which I am saved! Thank you for your baptism of the flesh as well as the spirit. I know I'm unworthy, but help me to strive to always do better, to be better, and to set an example for those around me. Help me lead them to the water, Lord.

Your Thoughts . . .

_____

_____

_____

_____

_____

_____

_____

_____

_____

_____

_____

_____

_____

_____

_____

_____

_____

_____

_____

_____

_____

_____

_____

_____

Sunday Thought:
A New Attitude

Whether giving thanks in joy
Or burdens need we share,
In everything we ought to bow
Our heads to God in prayer.

WHEN YOU BECOME A Christian, you get a new attitude. And while there are many virtues we ought to apply to our lives, a strong baseline is an attitude of prayer.

"Pray without ceasing" (1 Thessalonians 5:17, ESV).

We are instructed throughout the Bible regarding the many attitudes of prayer. First of all, we ought to be humble when addressing our Creator.

". . . God resists the proud, but gives grace to the humble" (1 Peter 5:5, NKJV).

I personally try to stay humble by first giving thanks before asking for anything; and this leads me to gratitude. We are exhorted to pray with a thankful heart.

"Continue in prayer, and watch in the same with thanksgiving" (Colossians 4:2, KJV).

First Thessalonians 5:18 says, "In every thing give thanks" (KJV); and I want to address this verse while I'm on the topic of gratitude. This does not mean that God expects us to thank him when awful things happen in our lives! He never wishes to see his children suffer. Rather, look at this verse as a reminder that there is always *something* to be grateful for, even under the worst circumstances.

Another important aspect of prayer is forgiveness. We are told to forgive others before we ourselves go to the Lord in prayer.

"'And whenever you stand praying, if you have anything against anyone, forgive him, that your Father in heaven may also forgive you your trespasses'" (Mark 11:25, NKJV).

I know from personal experience that this is much easier said than done! We have all had difficult situations in which we needed to forgive others. But rather than letting that discourage you, use it as an opportunity to grow. Forgiveness is in itself a surprisingly deep study; and we ought to pray to God for help in those situations as well.

God wants us to put our cares on his shoulders[1] and allow him to carry the burden; but this means we have to surrender ourselves to him in prayer. When Jesus himself prayed in Gethsemene before his crucifixion, he said, "O my Father, if it be possible, let this cup pass from me: nevertheless not as I will, but as thou wilt" (Matthew 26:39, KJV). We ought to follow this example in our own prayers, trusting that God alone can see the bigger picture.

Finally, we must have patience in prayer.[2] We don't always get the answer we want! But God knows all and sees all, and therefore his timing is perfect. We have to trust that God knows what he is about, and let our faith during life's trials be a true testimony to others.

"Wait on the LORD: be of good courage, and he shall strengthen thine heart: wait, I say, on the LORD" (Psalm 27:14, KJV).

Whether your prayers be long and thankful or short and distressed, make sure you approach God with the right attitude.

Heavenly Father, I thank you for the medium of prayer. Thank you for your promise to hear my pleas, and for the encouragement I get from your Word in my hour of need. Please help me to wait patiently for your answer, and trust that you have a plan.

1. 1 Peter 5:7
2. Psalm 37:7

Your Thoughts . . .

_____

_____

_____

_____

_____

_____

_____

_____

_____

_____

_____

_____

_____

_____

_____

_____

_____

_____

_____

_____

_____

_____

_____

_____

_____

_____

_____

_____

Sunday Thought:

Dealing With
Worldly Discouragement

The world will often bring you down
With all its evil ways
But stay the course and take the Lord
Along with you each day.

THIS WORLD DISCOURAGES ME daily, and I'm sure you've felt that way before too. But let me start by saying, we shouldn't flatter ourselves that this is the worst time in the world's history (as I have caught myself thinking on occasion). Bear in mind that there are 1,189 chapters in the Bible; and even back then, the world had become so corrupt that God destroyed it by chapter seven.

That being said, it can be difficult living in today's world. I have a hard time listening to the news, and even going out in public often tests me. Our senses are constantly assaulted: vulgarity and profanity are used in everyday language; homosexuality is not only tolerated but encouraged; and the news is filled with crimes against humanity and acts against God. We as Christians are often made to feel like outcasts—in a world where, once upon a time, you were looked at sideways if you *didn't* attend church.

As I sat down recently to read a devotion, I came upon the scripture that inspired me to write on this topic:

". . . For the things which are seen are temporary, but the things which are not seen are eternal" (2 Corinthians 4:18, NKJV).

This encourages me! And, while there are many beautiful things of the earth that I hope to see in Heaven, the things of the world I can do without.

There are many verses of encouragement in the Bible. We are told to trust in God,[1] reminded that our worldly troubles are momentary, and promised that our eternal glory will outweigh them all.[2]

". . . In the world you will have tribulation; but be of good cheer, I have overcome the world" (John 16:33, NKJV).

Let that powerful verse ground you when you're feeling discouraged.

Thank you, God, for your assurance that the evils of this world have no power over me. Sustain me, Lord, against the negativity, and help me instead to be a light to those still in the darkness, that they may see your light at the end of their path.

1. Proverbs 3:5
2. 2 Corinthians 4:17

Your Thoughts . . .

_____

_____

_____

_____

_____

_____

_____

_____

_____

_____

_____

_____

_____

_____

_____

_____

_____

_____

_____

_____

_____

_____

_____

_____

_____

_____

_____

_____

_____

Sunday Thought:
Being in the Minority

We often feel outnumbered,
But with Jesus on our side
How can we be the minority;
Who can conquer or divide?

THE WORLD TODAY PUSHES acceptance of everyone and everything, and we Christians are often made to feel like we are in the minority. In fact, this was said directly to me recently! But, instead of making me retract what I'd said that provoked this response, it kindled a fire in me—not to start trouble, but to stand up for what I think is right, even if I am in the minority.

And then I thought, if God is on my side, how can I ever be outnumbered?

"If God is for us, who can be against us?" (Romans 8:31, NKJV).

The Bible commands us not to do wrong just because the crowd does.[1] The world is fickle and ever-changing, and if we follow it, not only will we be led astray but we will never be satisfied.

". . . Do you not know that friendship with the world is enmity with God? Whoever therefore wants to be a friend of the world makes himself an enemy of God" (James 4:4, NKJV).

When we follow Jesus, we find not only salvation but true joy; the joy of the Spirit, which surpasses the evil of the world.

"'These things I have spoken to you, that My joy may remain in you, and that your joy may be full'" (John 15:11, NKJV).

The next time you are made to feel in the minority, remind yourself that God is on *your* side.

Dear Lord, I thank you for bolstering me up with your Word against the opposition of the world. Help me to stand out in a crowd and stay strong in my convictions, that your love might shine through me. Remind me, Lord, when I feel outnumbered, that you are on my side.

1. Ephesians 23:2

Your Thoughts . . .

_____

_____

_____

_____

_____

_____

_____

_____

_____

_____

_____

_____

_____

_____

_____

_____

_____

_____

_____

_____

_____

_____

_____

_____

_____

_____

_____

_____

Sunday Thought:
Clothing Ourselves with Christ

Stand firm with the belt of truth,
Take up the shield of faith
And all the armor of our God
Who saves us by his grace.

As CHRISTIANS, WE WANT to set a Christ-like example for others. What better way to do this than to clothe ourselves with him?

"Rather, clothe yourselves with the Lord Jesus Christ, and do not think about how to gratify the desires of the flesh" (Romans 13:14, NIV).

The Bible tells us to put on compassion, kindness, humility, gentleness, patience—and *love.*[1]

1. Colossians 3:12–14

". . . For whoever does not love their brother and sister, whom they have seen, cannot love God, whom they have not seen" (1 John 4:20, NIV).

When we live our lives by these virtues, we are putting on Christ.

This, of course, is easier said than done. But I would add here, while we're on the topic of clothing, that as I transitioned from the potty-mouthed road rager I used to be (sad but true), I began to wear clothes that represented my faith. Because it helped me to think twice, and remember who I was representing. And because people notice it.

So when you find yourself struggling with kindness, patience, or other Christ-like virtues, you may find that wearing faith-inspired clothing may just help you rise to the occasion as a representative of Jesus.

"Strength and honour are her clothing; and she shall rejoice in time to come" (Proverbs 31:25, KJV).

Dear God, thank you for giving me a new heart. Please guide me as I transform from the person I used to be into the person I want to be. Help me to know and remember your love, no matter what I've done in the past, and to always strive to do better.

Your Thoughts . . .

_____

_____

_____

_____

_____

_____

_____

_____

_____

_____

_____

_____

_____

_____

_____

_____

_____

_____

_____

_____

_____

_____

_____

_____

_____

_____

_____

_____

Sunday Thought:
On Relationships

We oughtn't to regard ourselves
As better than our brothers
But conversely, humility
Should be displayed to others.

I HAVE ALWAYS THOUGHT that the key to marital happiness is fairly simple: if each person puts the other one's needs before their own, then both husband and wife get put first. Sure, each person can prioritize themselves with a similar result, but isn't it better to be selfless, and then loved and appreciated in return?

The Bible confirms this theory on more than one occasion:

"Be devoted to one another in love. Honor one another above yourselves" (Romans 12:10, NIV).

"Do nothing from selfishness or empty conceit, but with humility consider one another as more important than yourselves" (Philippians 2:3, NASB).

These scriptures are not specific to marriage, but refer to the way in which Christians should regard all other people. But, if anything, this fact should make them even more relevant! Because Christian love should be woven into all of our relationships, whatever their nature.

So if you find yourself in a relationship that's lagging or feeling a bit one-sided, make sure your priorities are in order. Put Jesus first, then the other person, and yourself last. Even if you're the only one working on it, persevere in prayer and love, and let God's will be done.

Heavenly Father, I am grateful for the loved ones in my life. Please help me to maintain a humble spirit, putting others before myself so that they can feel your love through me.

Your Thoughts . . .

_____

_____

_____

_____

_____

_____

_____

_____

_____

_____

_____

_____

_____

_____

_____

Sunday Thought:

Forgiveness
Part I

Insomuch as in you lies,
Live at peace with men
Do not curse, but bless them;
Seek pardon, not revenge.

ABOUT A YEAR AGO I had a terrible fight with one of my sisters. Unfortunately, it was one of many over the years.

I prayed about it throughout the following week, but was so angry that I'm not sure I would have heard God if He'd answered. That Saturday night, somewhat calmer, I prayed about it again before going to sleep. The following morning when I opened my devotional (which I usually don't even do on Sundays), it stopped me in my tracks. The message was written in first person, unlike any of the previous ones. It read, *"Your sister wants me to remind you that she needs grace. Just like you need forgiveness, so does she."*[1]

When we pray, God listens.[2]

1. Lucado, *Grace For the Moment*, 256
2. 1 Peter 3:12

"This is the confidence we have in approaching God: that if we ask anything according to his will, he hears us" (1 John 5:14, NIV).

In this personal matter, I believe that God answered me only when he knew I would be receptive to it. When we cry out to God we must make sure we're listening for his answer, and remember to trust in his timing.

Dear God, I thank you for my family, and ask for your guidance when things go wrong between us. Grant me the wisdom to know what to say, and when to say nothing; and the patience to wait and listen when I ask for your help.

Your Thoughts . . .

_____

_____

_____

_____

_____

_____

_____

_____

_____

_____

_____

_____

_____

_____

_____

_____

_____

Sunday Thought:
Forgiveness
Part II

Forgive a man, less for his sake
And more for that of your own
Cleanse your heart, give it to God,
And leave well enough alone.

I STRUGGLED SO HARD with the situation with my sister
that I sought solitude for a few days in order to work on
forgiving her. We had tried to work it out, but in the process I got sucked in, responding to her accusations with
some of my own. And, while I had never said anything
that was untrue, I knew I should still ask for forgiveness—
both for the things she was upset with me for, and for
responding in anger.

But how? And how could I forgive someone who did
not even feel that she needed to be forgiven? I reached for
my Bible.

On dealing with anger:

"In your anger do not sin: Do not let the sun go down while you are still angry, and do not give the devil a foothold" (Ephesians 4:26–27, NIV).

On forgiving:

"Then Peter came to Him and said, 'Lord, how often shall my brother sin against me, and I forgive him? Up to seven times?' Jesus said to him, 'I do not say to you, up to seven times, but up to seventy times seven'" (Matthew 18:21–22, NKJV).

"For if you forgive men their trespasses, your Heavenly Father will also forgive you" (Matthew 6:14, NKJV).

On asking for forgiveness:

"Every way of a man is right in his own eyes, but the LORD weighs the hearts" (Proverbs 21:2, NKJV).

After two days of prayer and study I reached out to my sister, asking first for her forgiveness, and then offering mine.

Lord, it is hard to be forgiving. It's extremely difficult to ask for forgiveness when I feel like I'm the one who has been done wrong; but I must thank you for forgiving me for my own sins, and ask that you remind me of that undeserved grace when I struggle to forgive others. Help me to follow your example.

Your Thoughts . . .

_____

_____

_____

_____

_____

_____

_____

_____

_____

_____

_____

_____

_____

_____

_____

_____

_____

_____

_____

_____

_____

_____

_____

_____

_____

_____

_____

_____

_____

_____

_____

_____

Sunday Thought:
The Power of Prayer

We often times feel overwhelmed
With more than we can bear,
But never underestimate
The power of a prayer.

". . . THE prayer of a righteous person has great power as it is working" (James 5:16, ESV).

Everyone needs a boost now and then. Life is hard. For Christians, encouragement often comes in the form of answered prayer. I will use a personal example to illustrate this thought.

My husband works out of town. Consequently, he drives a lot, and I often pray for his safe travel to and from work. He was heading north toward home one night, and saw on the other side of the highway a southbound tractor-trailer that had broken down and was on fire. Just as he was directly across from it, a second semi heading south passed between them—and in that exact moment, the tires of the burning tractor-trailer exploded from the heat, launching burning debris everywhere.

Amazingly, no one was hurt; but had that semi not passed by at that precise moment, the burning debris would have shot directly at my husband, causing who knows how horrible an accident.

When we discussed it later, I commented that it's hard to understand how everything works. He could have been hurt or killed, and people do have accidents all the time.

Sometimes we don't get the answers to prayer that we're looking for, and sometimes we do. You can either chalk it up to chance, or you can have faith in the power of prayer, trusting that God knows the bigger picture. I choose the latter, and so does my husband. I told him that I had prayed for him just an hour or two before that near accident; and the following Sunday, he stood up in church and gave that testimony.

"Oh, give thanks to the Lord! Call upon His name; make known His deeds among the peoples!" (Psalm 105:1, NKJV).

Thank You, Father, for always answering my prayers! Help me to remain faithful when I don't get the answers that I hope for. Remind me, Lord, that the time of miracles has not passed; that you are alive and well, and always here when I need you.

Your Thoughts . . .

_____

_____

_____

_____

_____

_____

_____

_____

_____

_____

_____

_____

_____

_____

_____

_____

_____

_____

_____

_____

_____

_____

_____

_____

_____

_____

_____

Sunday Thought:
Why Do Bad Things
Happen to Good People?

Many are the things in life
We do not understand
But we must trust that by and by
We will—and til then, we rely
And hold to Jesus' hand.

IT'S ONE OF THE universal questions of this life, and is not easily answered. Why do bad things happen to good people? The best explanation I have ever heard is in the film adaptation of Janette Oke's *Love Comes Softly*:

The main character, when asked this question, replies: "My daughter can fall down and hurt herself, even if I'm walking right there beside her. But that doesn't mean I allowed it to happen. In all the moments of my life, God has been right there beside me. The truth of God's love isn't that he allows bad things to happen. It's his promise that he'll be there with us when they do."

"The eyes of the LORD are on the righteous, and His ears are open to their cry" (Psalm 34:15, NKJV).

We are told repeatedly in Ecclesiastes that chance is a part of life, whether it be bad or good. The Bible states that good fortune is not designated to the righteous, nor bad fortune to the wicked.[1]

We need to remember during our times of trial that everything works together for good for those who love the Lord,[2] even if we cannot see how at the time.

The story of Job also reminds us that we may be experiencing a test of our faith.[3] No matter the situation, God is there. He hears when we cry out to Him, and will comfort us in our grief.

"Blessed are those who mourn, for they shall be comforted" (Matthew 5:4, NKJV).

Oh God, life is so hard sometimes. Thank you for your promise that you are always with me, even in my darkest hour. Stay by my side, Lord, through life's trials and losses. Strengthen me with your Word, and help me to trust and obey.

Your Thoughts . . .

_____

_____

_____

_____

_____

1. Ecclesiastes 9

2. Romans 8:28

3. Job 1:6–22

Sunday Thought:
Forgive and Forget?

When we are wronged, we tend to forget
The grace by which we live.
It may be hard to forgive and forget,
But don't forget to forgive.

I CAN BE AS bad as anyone about holding a grudge. But, from a Christian perspective, shouldn't we forgive and forget? Let's start with Mark 11:25:

"But when you are praying, first forgive anyone you are holding a grudge against, so that your Father in Heaven will forgive your sins, too" (NLT).

We are told throughout Scripture to forgive others—even to pray for them.[1] However, the Bible does not actually contain the phrase 'forgive and forget;' nor are we exhorted to do so. That being said, Jesus forgave the most

1. Matthew 5:44

offensive of sinners throughout his life—even those who murdered him.[2] And we *are* instructed to be Christ-like.

"Let this mind be in you which was also in Christ Jesus" (Philippians 2:5, NKJV).

God is a forgiving God, and forgets about our sins once we have been forgiven.

"For I will be merciful to their unrighteousness, and their sins and their lawless deeds I will remember no more" (Hebrews 8:12, NKJV).

I believe that human nature prevents us from actually forgetting when we have been done wrong; and there is the point of wisdom in not forgetting the past, lest it repeat itself. But we ought to practice forgiveness, and be Christ-like in desiring mercy.[3]

Thank you, Father, for your mercy and forgiveness. Please give me strength when I struggle to let go of wrongs done against me. Help me to make wise decisions in my choice of friends, and to pray for those with whom I've had to part ways.

Your Thoughts . . .

_____

_____

_____

_____

_____

2. Luke 23:34
3. Hosea 6:6

Sunday Thought:
Resisting Temptation

Help me, Lord, to cleanse and purge
The workings of my mind
And rather than temptation there,
Your many blessings find.

WE HUMANS ENDURE MANY and varied forms of temptation, and for different reasons. Many people turn to substances, food, or sexual immorality as coping mechanisms, while others may resort to irresponsible purchases or even theft, for instant gratification. But this is where we need to know and remember that temptation is another aspect of humanity that Jesus can relate to.

"For we do not have a High Priest who cannot sympathize with our weaknesses, but was in all points tempted as we are, yet without sin" (Hebrews 4:15, NKJV).

When Jesus was tempted in the desert, he had fasted for forty days.[1] Then he was tempted by the devil himself,

1. Matthew 4:1–11

and managed to resist those promises of food, rest, and rule over all the kingdoms of the world.

It is still the devil tempting us today; he simply approaches us in the guises of physical satisfaction and material comfort, which are only temporary. We just need to remember that the sufferings of this world are also temporary.

"For our light affliction, which is but for a moment, is working for us a far more exceeding and eternal weight of glory" (2 Corinthians 4:17, NKJV).

God also promises that we will never be tempted beyond what we can handle:

"No temptation has overtaken you except such as is common to man; but God is faithful, who will not allow you to be tempted beyond what you are able, but with the temptation will also make the way of escape, that you may be able to bear it" (1 Corinthians 10:13, NKJV).

And a little more food for thought: the devil used Scripture to tempt Jesus! We Christians must be vigilant at all times, because he isn't always attacking in the ways we expect.[2]

Jesus resisted temptation, and ultimately, received from God all that had been promised him by the devil. He stayed the course and received his just reward. We too are strengthened and encouraged in our fight against the devil:

"Submit yourselves therefore to God. Resist the devil, and he will flee from you" (James 4:7, KJV).

2. 1 Peter 5:8–9

In following Jesus' example, we know that we will be rewarded in Heaven beyond anything we can imagine or hope for.[3]

"Blessed is the man who endures temptation; for when he has been approved, he will receive the crown of life which the Lord has promised to those who love Him" (James 1:12, NKJV).

Dear Lord, please guide me in your ways. Help me to remember that these days of temptation are only temporary, and that a glory awaits your children which will surpass any worldly obstacles! Thank you for the encouragement I find in your Word.

Your Thoughts . . .

_____

_____

_____

_____

_____

_____

_____

_____

_____

_____

_____

_____

_____

_____

_____

3. Matthew 5:12

Sunday Thought:

Gethsemene

Prayed Jesus in that darkest hour,
"Not my will, but Thine."
Surely we can say as much
In our own troubled time.

JESUS PRAYED IN GETHSEMANE before his crucifixion:

"My Father, if it be possible, let this cup pass from me; yet not as I will, but as You will" (Matthew 26:39, NIV).

Jesus was a man. A human; yet he lived a perfect life. This can be hard to wrap our heads around, but we are told in Scripture that he suffered temptation, hunger, and other trials, just as we do. And there are many instances in the Bible where this point is illustrated. I believe that when Jesus prayed that night in Gethsemane, he was demonstrating that, though he was a God-man who never faltered in his faith, he did feel the human emotions of fear and dread. Perhaps he prayed that night so that his mortal fear could one day bring us comfort in our own.

It is okay to ask God to "let this cup pass from me." Just because we have a moment of fear doesn't mean that we aren't trusting God. It means we're human. We just need to stay humble and trust in the Lord, praying that his will be done.

"And we know that all things work together for good to those who love God . . ." (Romans 8:28, NKJV).

Heavenly Father, I thank you for sending Jesus, a Savior who understands my human heart. Please help me to trust you through my trials and doubts, that I might grow in faith and set an example for others who might be struggling.

Your Thoughts . . .

_____

_____

_____

_____

_____

_____

_____

_____

_____

_____

_____

_____

_____

_____

_____

_____

_____

_____

Sunday Thought:
The Sparrow

As little birds must learn to fly
So we must learn to trust,
And as their songs impart such joy
Does God bring joy to us!

In the summer of 2023, I had an amazing experience rescuing, and subsequently bonding with, a wild animal. My husband spotted a fledgling purple martin on the ground in our yard, which had either fallen or been pushed too early from the nest. I knew it was an undertaking to rescue it, but I also knew that my cats would kill it if we didn't. So, I scooped it up and proceeded to care for it for the next two weeks.

I had the privilege of hand-feeding a baby bird and gaining its trust. I called it Martin (though she ended up being female); and that bird responded to my voice, learned her name, and would lay on my shoulder or in my hair. She actually enjoyed car rides; and once she learned to fly, there was no stopping her from coming to me every chance she got.

Fortunately, this story only has a sad ending for me. Remember those cats I mentioned? Well, I'm pretty sure they had a contract out on the bird, bless her ignorant little heart. So, once I knew that Martin had flown and hunted with the other martins on our property, I released her at the home of an acquaintance who also had purple martin houses. And, as much as it broke my heart, Martin flew on the first attempt, which told me she would be okay.

Martin put smiles on a lot of people's faces with her antics, and I'll never forget her. It certainly gave new meaning to Matthew 10:29!

"Are not two sparrows sold for a farthing? And one of them shall not fall on the ground without your Father" (Matthew 10:29, KJV).

This little bird literally fell to the ground, and somehow we found her before my bird-killing cats did. It could be a coincidence . . . or, maybe God knew what joy that bird would bring to my heart. Maybe he knew it would put a smile on the face of an elderly woman who was having a hard time; or that it would teach some children about nurturing even the smallest life.

I prefer to think the latter.

If God cares this much for the smallest of creatures, imagine how much he loves us, his own children.

". . . Fear not therefore; ye are of more value than many sparrows" (Luke 12:7, KJV).

Dear God, I am grateful for all of the blessings you have bestowed upon me, down to the smallest one. Thank you for the reminder of how much you care about me.

Your Thoughts . . .

_____

_____

_____

_____

_____

_____

_____

_____

_____

_____

_____

_____

_____

_____

_____

_____

_____

_____

_____

_____

_____

_____

_____

_____

_____

_____

_____

_____

Sunday Thought:
Dealing With Negativity

Lord, please save me from myself
And grant a peaceful mind
That I, through all the fear and doubt,
Your blessings may divine.

I AM GENERALLY A happy person, but I often struggle with negativity. More specifically, if some event is approaching where I'm unsure of the outcome, I tend to dread the negative possible outcomes, assuming the worst—and before I know it, I'm worked up over something that hasn't even happened. (Yet. I mean, it still could.)

But seriously, the point is that I know better! Getting back to church and Christian fellowship, and studying and praying has helped me tremendously with this. Let's see what the Bible has to say about it.

"Therefore do not worry about tomorrow, for tomorrow will worry about its own things. Sufficient for the day is its own trouble" (Matthew 6:34, NKJV).

Amen to that. Why borrow trouble from tomorrow, which we can't do anything about, when there is plenty to deal with today, which we can deal with now?

Paul also admonished the Corinthians to ". . . take captive every thought to make it obedient to Christ" (2 Corinthians 10:5, NIV).

So, wouldn't this include negative thoughts? This of course is easier said than done; but this is where we should meditate on it. There is a difference in reading a verse and studying it . . . but that will be a separate thought for another Sunday.

Lastly, we should pray about it—or, actually, we should start with that!

"Do not be anxious about anything, but in every situation, by prayer and petition, with thanksgiving, present your requests to God" (Philippians 4:6, NIV).

We are told to pray in *every* situation. One day I was having a morning that was so off, I prayed about it and never even said amen; I just left it open-ended. Fortunately, it was a Sunday morning, and if I'm down I always feel better after church.

If you're like me and you struggle with negativity, I hope you will take some time to consider these verses.

Lord, you know the workings of my mind. I thank you for the strength of your Word, and ask that you continue to bolster me up against the negative thoughts that try to destroy my peace.

Your Thoughts . . .

_____
_____
_____
_____
_____
_____
_____
_____
_____
_____
_____
_____
_____
_____
_____
_____
_____
_____
_____
_____
_____
_____
_____
_____
_____
_____

Sunday Thought:
In a Word

Jesus' death upon the cross
Was suffering beyond words;
A new one was invented
To describe what he endured.

DID YOU KNOW THAT Jesus' suffering on the cross was so appalling, a new word was invented in order to describe it? I learned this while reading Lee Strobel's *The Case for Christ*, which I highly recommend.

Excruciate: *To torture, torment, inflict very severe pain on*

The word "excruciate" derives from the word "excruciare," which means "as painful as a crucifixion," or, "from/out the cross." The Romans invented this word, as the agony of crucifixion was so intense that there had previously existed no word to describe it.

Jesus was betrayed,[1] accused and judged, flogged (a horror in itself), humiliated, and pushed beyond physical

1. Luke 22:48

endurance. He had a crown of thorns driven into his head.[2] Then he was laid upon the cross, and metal spikes (I think of railroad ties) were driven through his wrists, nailing him to it. Another nail was driven through his ankles.

He was raised into the air, and I imagine a terrible jarring, as the cross would presumably have been dropped into a hole in the ground to keep it upright. The moment this happened, the weight of Jesus' body would have sagged with gravity, meaning that for every single breath, he must push up against the nail in his ankles and pull down against the ones in his hands, in order to lift himself to take a breath. For three hours he endured this suffering, slowly suffocating, until at last he gave up the ghost.

"Jesus called out in a loud voice, 'Father, into your hands I commit my spirit.' When He had said this, He breathed His last" (Luke 23:46, NIV).

This is some of what Jesus endured for us. The purpose of this perfect sacrifice was for the salvation of mankind: for me, and for you. Jesus' crucifixion brought an end to the Old Testament animal sacrifices for the atonement of sin; that's why Jesus is often called the Lamb.

Excruciate. Not many words carry such meaning.

"For God so loved the world that He gave His only begotten Son, that whoever believes in Him should not perish but have everlasting life" (John 3:16, NKJV).

The Four Gospel accounts of the crucifixion:

2. Matthew 27:29

Matthew 27:32–54
Mark 15:21–38
Luke 23:26–47
John 19:16–30

Dear Jesus, I thank you for your blood which was spilt for me; for your body that was broken for me; and for your life, which was cut short so that mine might last forever. Thank you for your perfect sacrifice.

Your Thoughts . . .

Sunday Thought:
Giving God the Glory

May we accept life's challenges
According to his will
And as the tempest at the eye,
Be mollified and still.

"FOR YOU WERE BOUGHT at a price; therefore glorify God in your body and in your spirit, which are God's" (1 Corinthians 6:20, NKJV).

Bethany Hamilton was just a girl from Hawaii who aspired to be a surfer. Then in 2003, at age 13, she was attacked by a shark which bit off her entire arm. Amazingly, however, she was soon back in the water.

Bethany has since realized not only her dream of becoming a professional surfer, but of becoming a wife and mother as well. Best of all, this brave woman gives the glory to God. She has inspired countless people with her determination, perseverance, and Christian faith.

For me, her story gives new meaning to 1 Corinthians 10:31:

"Therefore, whether you eat or drink, or whatever you do, do all to the glory of God" (NKJV).

This brave woman faces a challenge in each of the daily tasks that most of us take for granted as simple. To maintain her faith through such a traumatic event (and at such a tender age), and then overcome the disability it left her with to live a normal life, is an outstanding testimony!

When we submit to God's will[3] the burdens of this life are easier to bear, no matter how heavy the load. And when we give him the glory, the victories are so much sweeter!

"Let your light so shine before men, that they may see your good works, and glorify your Father which is in heaven" (Matthew 5:16, KJ21).

NOTE: Bethany Hamilton shares her testimony in her memoir *Soul Surfer*, which has been made into a film of the same title.

Dear God, please help me as I strive to glorify you in all things. Thank you for the promise that you will sustain me, Lord, so that when the going gets tough, those around me will see you shining through and working in my life.

3. James 4:7

Your Thoughts . . .

_____

_____

_____

_____

_____

_____

_____

_____

_____

_____

_____

_____

_____

_____

_____

_____

_____

_____

_____

_____

_____

_____

_____

_____

_____

_____

_____

_____

Sunday Thought:
God Counts Your Tears

Jesus knew what it was to mourn,
To feel the pain of grief;
He understands the tears of those
To whom he'll bring relief

"YOU HAVE KEPT COUNT of my tossings; put my tears in your bottle. Are they not in your book?" (Psalm 56:8, ESV).

When Jesus' beloved friend Lazarus had died and he saw the grief of the other mourners, Jesus wept.[1] But soon afterward, he resurrected Lazarus from the dead. We need to ask ourselves, why did Jesus mourn for his friend when it was his intention all along to bring him back to life?[2]

Because Jesus empathized with the mourners![3] He hurt because they hurt, and wept with those who wept.[4]

1. John 11:35
2. John 11:23
3. John 11:33
4. Romans 12:15

We endure a lot of grief in this life; but because Jesus lived a mortal life, he understands our tears. Just as he was with the mourners of Lazarus, Jesus is with us in all our moments of grief. When we live our lives for him we know that he will sustain us, and that one day there will be no more tears.[5]

"And God will wipe away every tear from their eyes; there shall be no more death, nor sorrow, nor crying. There shall be no more pain, for the former things have passed away" (Revelation 21:4, NKJV).

Dear Jesus, I thank you for leaving the right hand of God to live a mortal life, that you might understand what I feel and go through. Help me to remember your experiences when I struggle through my own!

Your Thoughts . . .

_____
_____
_____
_____
_____
_____
_____
_____
_____
_____
_____
_____
_____

5. Isaiah 25:8

Sunday Thought:
Reading vs. Studying

Study to show thyself approved,
A worker amongst men;
For a scripture worth the writing down
Is worth a look again.

"THY WORD IS A lamp unto my feet, and a light unto my path" (Psalm 119:105, KJV).

There is a difference in reading the Bible, and actually studying it. There are many Scriptures that can easily be misunderstood—or overlooked completely—by not taking the time to meditate on and truly comprehend them.

One example would be 1 John 3:9: "No one who has been born of God practices sin . . ." (NASB).

This would probably make some people snap their Bibles shut and walk away. But if we take the time to study the rest of this verse, we learn that here, "practice" means to do *continually*. As in, to persist in a sinful way of life, as opposed to having a weak moment and slipping up (which we all do).

"No one who has been born of God practices sin, because His seed remains in him; and he cannot sin continually because he has been born of God" (1 John 3:9, NASB).

This verse isn't telling us that children of God don't sin, or that we're condemned if we do. If that were the case Jesus' sacrifice would be null and void, because we all sin, even the best of us. Therefore we are saved by grace, through faith.[1]

As an aside, our pastor puts a lot of emphasis on context, and I will point that out here as well. Many well-known verses are quoted only in part (1 Peter 3:15, Romans 8:28, etc), and it's always worthwhile to read them in full. Moreover, it never hurts to go back and read the preceding verses, or even the whole chapter, to put a verse into context and better understand it.

God promises wisdom to the faithful who ask for it.[2]

Heavenly Father, I am so grateful for the leading and instruction of your Word. Guide me in my studies, granting me spiritual discernment that I may continue to learn, grow, and understand your will for my life.

1. Ephesians 2:8–9
2. James 1:5

Your Thoughts . . .

_____

_____

_____

_____

_____

_____

_____

_____

_____

_____

_____

_____

_____

_____

_____

_____

_____

_____

_____

_____

_____

_____

_____

_____

_____

_____

_____

Sunday Thought:

A Leap of Faith

Help me, Lord, to walk by faith
And shine your light for others
That one day they may truly be
My sisters and my brothers

WHAT IS FAITH, EXACTLY? This study is a deep one—but let's get to root of it:

"Now faith is the substance of things hoped for, the evidence of things not seen" (Hebrews 11:1, KJV).

God sacrificed his only Son for the remission of our sins. Because of this sacrifice, we are no longer condemned to hell for our sins when we die. But, God gives us the free will to make that decision for ourselves. We must invite him into our lives and accept that gift of salvation, if we are to spend eternity with him in heaven.

When you get saved, the Holy Spirit comes to dwell within you.[1] Pause for a moment and take that in: the

1. 1 Corinthians 6:19

same Spirit who raised Christ from the dead comes to live within *you*.[2] This is not just positive thinking, or any other term that is easily dismissed. It is an experience of faith, unique to each person who lives for God. We don't always understand God's will, or get the answers to prayer that we're hoping for. But our prayers will and *do* get answered.[3]

Some things simply cannot be expressed in words. In that, don't just take me at mine. Take that leap of faith for yourself. Invite Jesus into your life, and let God speak to you.

"For we walk by faith, not by sight" (2 Corinthians 5:7, NKJV).

"So then faith comes by hearing, and hearing by the word of God" (Romans 10:17, NKJV).

Dear God, help me to take that leap of faith each and every day. Bolster me up with your Word, and convict me with your Spirit, who lives within me. Help me to grow in faith through life's trials, and not waver.

Your Thoughts . . .

_____

_____

_____

_____

_____

_____

_____

2. Romans 8:11

3. 1 John 5:14

Sunday Thought:
Looking Through the Curves

Trust in the Lord, for the gate is narrow
And difficult the way
Lean on him, and he will guide
Through curves that come your way.

"YOU ARE MY HIDING place; you will protect me from trouble and surround me with songs of deliverance" (Psalm 32:7, NIV).

My husband and I love to ride our motorcycles. When a person is learning to ride, they are taught to look through the curves in order to anticipate the right angle of approach. This means taking their eyes *off* of the road in front of them, to look ahead instead. This is to keep the rider's focus off of their front wheel and on any upcoming hazards. If there is a tight curve coming up, it can mean turning your head completely.

This is hard to do! And it recently occurred to me that living a Christian life is a similar concept. Sometimes there are bends in the road where we can't see what's coming; but rather than worry ourselves off track, we should pray for guidance[4] and have faith that we will be delivered safely through, knowing that God can see the bigger picture.

"Trust in the Lord with all your heart and lean not on your own understanding; in all your ways submit to him, and he will make your paths straight" (Proverbs 3:5–6, NIV).

Dear God, I thank you for your promise to be with me through all of life's trials. Help me to keep the faith through the difficult times as well as the good, trusting in your will and your plan for my life.

Your Thoughts . . .

_____

_____

_____

_____

_____

_____

_____

_____

_____

_____

_____

_____

_____

_____

_____

_____

4. Philippians 4:6

Sunday Thought:

The Way of All Flesh

The way of flesh is too the way
The soul shall go that on that day
Of judgement is found still in want;
So tarry not, do not delay!

"FOR THE LIVING KNOW that they will die . . ." (Ecclesiastes 9:5, ESV).

You and I know that one day we will pass away; death is inevitable. But we do not have to be afraid of it. I think that even Christians, if we're being honest, will admit that the idea of dying *is* a little scary—because it is unknown to us. But Jesus, who lived a mortal life (as we do) and died (as we will), conquered death; and we need to remember that because of his perfect sacrifice, we too have victory over death!

"Most assuredly, I say to you, he who hears My word and believes in Him who sent Me has everlasting life, and shall not come into judgement, but has passed from death into life" (John 5:24, NKJV).

"But we do not want you to be uninformed, brothers, about those who are asleep, that you may not grieve as others do who have no hope. For since we believe that Jesus died and rose again, even so, through Jesus, God will bring with him those who have fallen asleep" (1 Thessalonians 4:13–14, ESV).

And when we do grieve the loss of a loved one, God knows it. He is always with us, counting our very tears:

"You keep track of all my sorrows. You have collected all my tears in your bottle. You have recorded each one in your book" (Psalm 56:8, NLT).

Last summer, one of my great-uncles passed away. And, though the funeral was of course sad, I was also encouraged by it. My uncle was a godly man, and because of his faith, this gathering of mourners was also a celebration of life—as it should be! You can know where you're going when you die, thereby granting peace of mind, not only for yourself but for the loved ones you leave behind.

". . . Death is the funeral of all our sorrows."
—Thomas J. Watson, *A Body of Divinity*

Those who serve the Lord need not fear death. Indeed, we should desire to feel as Paul did in his letter to the Philippians:

"For to me to live is Christ, and to die is gain" (Philippians 1:21, KJV).

Death does not have to mean the scythe of the Grim Reaper. It can mean the arms of Jesus!

Heavenly Father, I thank you for your words of comfort in my times of sorrow. Thank you for the gift of salvation, and for the peace of mind in knowing what awaits me when I die, so that I need not live in fear. Help me to always remember your promise.

Your Thoughts . . .

_____

_____

_____

_____

_____

_____

_____

_____

_____

_____

_____

_____

_____

_____

_____

_____

_____

_____

_____

_____

_____

_____

_____

Sunday Thought:
The Best Medicine

When we need unburdened from the troubles that we bear,
The only better remedy than laughter is a prayer.

WE'VE ALL HEARD THAT laughter is the best medicine. Like so many expressions we use today, this saying originated from the Bible.

"A merry heart does good, like medicine . . ." (Proverbs 17:22, NKJV).

The beatitudes in Ecclesiastes tell us that there is a time to weep and a time to laugh;[1] and in the Gospel of Luke, mourners are encouraged this way as well:

". . . Blessed are you who weep now, for you shall laugh" (Luke 6:21, NKJV).

1. Ecclesiastes 3:4

But, while laughter can certainly help relieve our feelings, we are reminded in Proverbs that this is only a temporary comfort:

"Even in laughter the heart may sorrow, and the end of mirth may be grief" (Proverbs 14:13, NKJV).

We need to remember that the true way to healing is through Jesus.[2]

"He heals the brokenhearted and binds up their wounds" (Psalm 147:3, NKJV).

Whenever we need healing, we need to turn to God in prayer. As much as I love to laugh, it doesn't compare to the peace I get from talking things over with God. No matter how tough life gets, there will always be his promise at the end of it.

"O LORD my God, I cried out to You, and You healed me" (Psalm 30:2, NKJV).

Thank you, Lord, for the joy of laughter, which helps relieve my feelings. But more importantly, I'm grateful that I can always come to you in prayer. Thank you for listening and caring, and for your promise that you will always answer.

2. Psalm 119:50

Your Thoughts . . .

Sunday Thought:

Crying Out to God

When we endure life's trials
God knows and feels our pain
And listens when we call to him;
Take not his name in vain.

WHETHER YOU KNOW IT or not, I guarantee that you have cried out to God at some point in your life. Many people claim not to know God, or even to believe in him: yet, what does a person do when they find themselves in imminent danger?

They pray for help.

Likewise, when someone is immensely relieved, they breathe out, "Thank God."

When people learn that they don't have long to live, they often go searching for God.

. . . You get my point.

God wants to be there for us. But he does not want to be saved for a rainy day, and then pushed aside again until the next emergency. He wants us to cry out to him in all situations.[3]

". . . O Judah, what shall I do to you? For your faithfulness is like a morning cloud, and like the early dew it goes away" (Hosea 6:4, NKJV).

Don't wait until you're facing your own mortality. Keep God close during the good times as well as the bad; then when trouble comes, you will already know that you're not alone, and that your prayers will be heard and answered.[4]

"The righteous cry out, and the Lord hears, and delivers them out of all their troubles" (Psalm 34:17, NKJV).

Oh Lord, thank you for always hearing my cries! Help me to put aside my pride and call on you in my hour of distress, trusting that you understand my needs, and will know what's best.

Your Thoughts . . .

_____
_____
_____
_____
_____
_____
_____
_____

3. Philippians 4:6
4. Isaiah 65:24

Sunday Thought:
The Begats

Oh come, thou Rod of Jesse,
Thou son of David, come!
That I, a child of Abraham,
Might reach my heavenly home.

THROUGHOUT THE BIBLE, THERE are lengthy accounts of family lineage. (Abraham begot Isaac, Isaac begot Jacob, etc.) These are tedious to read through, and I'm sure I'm not the first person to skip over them at times. I fondly refer to them as "the begats."

Last year I started reading in Matthew, and had read only one verse before—you guessed it—the begats! Fifteen verses of them.

I powered through, from Abraham to Joseph; and, though I didn't recall many of the generations listed, reading them reminded me of some familial biblical connections I had forgotten. It also prompted a question, which led to more study:

Why does Matthew's account record the lineage of Jesus through his adopted father (Joseph) rather than through his birth mother (Mary)?

. . . More study.

There is another genealogy in Luke, this one branching off through a different son of David. Here we have found Jesus' royal lineage through Mary.

At that time, family histories were recorded through the male line, which explains why in Matthew, Joseph is said to be begot of Jacob (his father);[1] and in Luke, he is said to be of Heli (his father-in-law).[2]

Mary and Joseph were both descended from David (through different sons), thus fulfilling beyond a doubt the prophecy of the Messiah through the line of David:

"Behold, the days come, saith the LORD, that I will raise unto David a righteous Branch, and a King shall reign and prosper, and shall execute judgment and justice in the earth" (Jeremiah 23:5, KJV).

The moral of the story? Read your Bible, because there is always more to learn—even from the begats!

Thank you for your Word, Lord, which always teaches me something new. Guide me in my studies, that I might continue to know you better and understand your ways.

1. Matthew 1:16
2. Luke 3:23

Your Thoughts . . .

_____

_____

_____

_____

_____

_____

_____

_____

_____

_____

_____

_____

_____

_____

_____

_____

_____

_____

_____

_____

_____

_____

_____

_____

_____

_____

_____

_____

Sunday Thought:
Paying for Convenience

We get what he paid for.

IN OUR DAY-TO-DAY LIVES, we pay for convenience: fast food that is already prepared, running through a car wash instead of doing it ourselves, buying a chicken at the grocery store that has already been killed, prepared, and cooked. Even shredded cheese costs more than unshredded.

The point is, convenience is simpler—just like living for the world is less complicated than living for God. It's easier to give up than it is to put on the armor of God and go to battle;[1] or to cry about your pain to a friend than to cry out to God for comfort.

But, just like we do when buying groceries, those of the world will pay for the convenience—but on a much larger scale.[2]

1. Ephesians 6:10–20
2. John 12:48, Revelation 21:8

"He who rejects Me, and does not receive My words, has that which judges him—the word that I have spoken will judge him in the last day" (John 12:48, NKJV).

It is not worth an eternity of torment for a few fleeting years of convenience.

Dear Lord, help me to always remember the price you paid for my salvation. Thank you for all you have done, and continue to do in my daily life. Thank you for walking with me.

Your Thoughts . . .

_____

_____

_____

_____

_____

_____

_____

_____

_____

_____

_____

_____

_____

_____

_____

_____

_____

_____

_____

_____

Sunday Thought:
Big Brother

Jesus, Lamb of Sacrifice
You love me like no other
You are the King, the Lord of lords,
My Savior and my brother.

I GREW UP ONE of four girls; but when I was little, I always wanted a big brother. (I still remember the disappointment when it finally dawned on me that this was an impossibility.)

Christians often refer to one another as "brother" or "sister," because we are all children of God. But it was the longest time before it occurred to me to think of Jesus as our older brother. I studied the subject, and the Bible refers to Jesus as our brother in more than one instance.

So, not only is Jesus our Lord and Savior, but our brother as well. I am reminded of the old hymn, "Jesus Is All the World to Me."

"For both He who sanctifies and those who are sanctified are all from one Father; for this reason He is not ashamed to call them brothers and sisters" (Hebrews 2:11, NASB).

"For whom He foreknew, He also predestined to be conformed to the image of His Son, that He might be the firstborn among many brethren" (Romans 8:29, NKJV).

. . . I always wanted a big brother.

Thank you, God, for your Son. He is my Savior, my friend, my Lord, and my brother. I am so grateful to know that he understands.

Your Thoughts . . .

_____

_____

_____

_____

_____

_____

_____

_____

_____

_____

_____

_____

_____

_____

_____

_____

_____

_____

_____

_____

Sunday Thought:
Praying For the Little Things

Matters of little consequence
To one, mean much to another
If it matters to you, it matters to God;
Take all of your cares to the Father.

I HAVE ALWAYS FELT that in a marriage, little things are big things. I like to share with my husband not only my heavy burdens, but also my minor, day to day concerns. This way he can share the burden, and help reassure me.

We should have the same attitude in our relationship with God. He wants to hear about all of our little worries and concerns—not just the big ones. In Philippians 4:6, we are told to pray to God in every situation; and in the following verse, we're assured that he will grant us peace.

At church, it can be difficult to ask for prayer to get over a cold when the person in the next pew is coping with cancer. And it might be hard to pray for guidance in a decision about your employment, when your neighbor has just lost his job.

But, while it is good to stay humble and count your blessings, don't let this stop you from praying for your own needs and concerns! They are no less important to God.

"You keep track of all my sorrows" (Psalm 56:8, NLT).

The next time you find yourself hesitating to pray about something "little," remind yourself that God cares about that, too. He is willing to share the burden—whether you're coping with illness, struggling financially, or worried about a pet that has wandered off.

"Be anxious for nothing, but in everything by prayer and supplication, with thanksgiving, let your requests be made known to God " (Philippians 4:6, NKJV).

Dear God, thank you for caring about even my smallest concerns! Thank you for the comfort of your Word, and the assurance of prayer. Help me to remember to turn to you in all things.

Your Thoughts . . .

_____

_____

_____

_____

_____

_____

_____

_____

Sunday Thought:
Telling Stories

Your life is a story that others will read
So be sure to give it a moral.
Live so that when your tale comes to an end,
Others celebrate rather than sorrow.

JESUS OFTEN TAUGHT THROUGH parables, which are stories from daily life that teach a spiritual truth. In fact, about a third of Jesus' teachings were conveyed in this way.

I believe that he still likes to teach through stories—ours! There are many stories in the Bible about people being drawn to Jesus by the Christian testimony of others; and I believe it is our duty to carry the torch in today's world. Our Christian testimonies are *our* stories, and we should tell them and live them. We never know who's watching and listening, or who might be drawn to Christ by our examples.

"Many Samaritans from that town believed in him because of the woman's testimony, 'He told me everything I ever did'" (John 4:39, NIV).

If you are a Christian and God has worked in your life, then you have a testimony. So think about it; and don't keep the joy to yourself, or hide the light under the proverbial bush.[1] Tell your family, tell your friends—heck, tell strangers! And, most importantly, live your words.

"But be doers of the word, and not hearers only, deceiving yourselves" (James 1:22, NKJV).

Thank you, God, for all of the stories in Scripture that teach me so much. Help me to lead a life that tells a story others can learn from.

Your Thoughts . . .

_____

_____

_____

_____

_____

_____

_____

_____

_____

_____

_____

_____

_____

_____

_____

_____

1. Matthew 5:16

Sunday Thought:

The Inner Room

Jesus knows our very hearts
And what we are about,
So be certain the inside of you
Matches with the out.

IN LUKE CHAPTER 18, we read Jesus' parable of the Phari-
see and the tax collector:

> "'Two men went up to the temple to pray, one
> a Pharisee and the other a tax collector. The
> Pharisee stood by himself and prayed: 'God, I
> thank you that I am not like other people—rob-
> bers, evildoers, adulterers—or even like this tax
> collector. I fast twice a week and give a tenth of
> all I get.'
>
> "But the tax collector stood at a distance.
> He would not even look up to heaven, but beat
> his breast and said, 'God, have mercy on me, a
> sinner.'
>
> "I tell you that this man, rather than the
> other, went home justified before God. For all
> those who exalt themselves will be humbled,

and those who humble themselves will be ex-
alted'" (Luke 18:10–14, NIV).

The Christian walk is not about what we do "out
loud." It's not about attending services three times a week,
but about having a personal relationship with God. It's
about worshiping him in our hearts, whether we're in a
chapel or at home, and in whatever we are doing.

"Therefore, whether you eat or drink, or whatever
you do, do all to the glory of God" (1 Corinthians 10:31,
NKJV).

It's not about how much money we put in the offering plate, but about being a joyful giver,[1] whether our
contribution is substantial or a widow's offering.[2]

And it's not about public good works, but what we
do in private; how we serve others, and the way live our
lives.

We are exhorted to be just, love mercy, and walk
humbly with God.[3]

"But when you pray, go into your room, close the
door and pray to your Father, who is unseen. Then your
Father, who sees what is done in secret, will reward you"
(Matthew 6:6, NIV).

*Heavenly Father, please help me to maintain a gener-
ous attitude and a humble spirit. Help me to set a good example for others, and to always strive to do, and be, better.*

1. 2 Corinthians 9:7
2. Mark 12:41–44
3. Micah 6:8

SUNDAY THOUGHTS

Your Thoughts . . .

_____
_____
_____
_____
_____
_____
_____
_____
_____
_____
_____
_____
_____
_____
_____
_____
_____
_____
_____
_____
_____
_____
_____
_____
_____
_____

Sunday Thought:
Good Luck?

Some say "good luck," but others say
This is irreverence
How do we know what is God's will
And what's coincidence?

SOME CHRISTIANS THINK THAT it's irreverent to wish someone "good luck," owing to the Christian doctrine of predestination, and everything being God's will. Personally, I have never been able to synchronize the concepts of free will and predestination; and I attended a ladies' day last year where the guest speaker addressed this very issue. She pointed out Ecclesiastes 9:11:

"I again saw under the sun that the race is not to the swift and the battle is not to the warriors, and neither is bread to the wise nor wealth to the discerning, nor favor to the skillful; for time and chance overtake them all" (NASB).

Upon further research, I find that most scriptures regarding predestination refer to us being predestined to be children of God.[1]

"For whom He foreknew, He also predestined to be conformed to the image of His Son, that He might be the firstborn among many brethren" (Romans 8:29, KJ21).

But whether we choose this path is another matter . . . which brings us to free will. We are told in Scripture that the Lord has made everything for its own purpose.[2] I myself don't think this means that every act or situation is predestined, but rather, that God *uses* each of these scenarios for a higher purpose, when we invite him into our lives. (Again, free will.) We are also assured that all things work together for good to those who love God.[3]

There is always plenty of room for more study, but at the end of the day I don't think there's anything wrong with wishing a person good luck.

God, sometimes things happen that I just don't understand. Please help me during these trials, to trust that you know the bigger picture and will work it all together for good. Work your will into my life, Lord.

1. Ephesians 1:5, Romans 8:29
2. Proverbs 16:4
3. Romans 8:28

Your Thoughts . . .

_____

_____

_____

_____

_____

_____

_____

_____

_____

_____

_____

_____

_____

_____

_____

_____

_____

_____

_____

_____

_____

_____

_____

_____

_____

_____

_____

_____

_____

Sunday Thought:
Go Tell John

We each experience moments of doubt,
But what matters more than these
Is emerging stronger on the other side
And trusting assuredly.

JOHN THE BAPTIST WAS born to prepare the way for the Messiah.[1] He was also Jesus' cousin. We are told that when Mary visited Elizabeth while they were both pregnant, Elizabeth's child leapt in the womb.[2]

But even John questioned Jesus in later years, when he was imprisoned and his days were numbered:

> "And when John had heard in prison about the works of Christ, he sent two of his disciples and said to Him, 'Are You the Coming One, or do we look for another?'
>
> "Jesus answered and said to them, 'Go and tell John the things which you hear and see: The blind see and the lame walk; the lepers are

1. Luke 1:17
2. Luke 1:41–42

cleansed and the deaf hear; the dead are raised up and the poor have the gospel preached to them'" (Matthew 11:2–5, NKJV).

It is okay to question our faith. In fact, I would venture to say that most of us do at times—particularly when we are under duress, as John was. Questions lead to deeper study; and when we seek God, he makes his presence known.

"I love those who love me, and those who seek me diligently will find me" (Proverbs 8:17, NKJV).

Lord, forgive me in my moments of doubt. Help me to seek you first when I feel weak, that I may grow ever stronger in my faith. Thank you for your promise that if I look for you, I will find you.

Your Thoughts . . .

_____

_____

_____

_____

_____

_____

_____

_____

_____

_____

_____

_____

_____

Sunday Thought:
Get Right, Church!

Are they words on a page, or inspiration?
Is it ritual, or way of life?
If your heart is not where it ought to be,
Talk to Jesus and get right!

GOING TO CHURCH SHOULDN'T be something we dread, but something we look forward to. It shouldn't mean fighting to stay awake during the sermon, but rather, letting God into your heart and opening yourself up to his Word.

Attending church should have you leaving the chapel more encouraged than when you walked in. I say "chapel" because the church is the *people*. We need to remember that.

"For as we have many members in one body, but all the members do not have the same function, so we, being many, are one body in Christ, and individually members of one another" (Romans 12:4–5, NKJV).

Go to church, and learn the difference between happiness of the flesh and the true joy of the Spirit. It is God's plan that we live life with an attitude of love,[1] having a peaceful mind and a song in our heart.[2]

"For God has not given us a spirit of fear, but of power and of love and of a sound mind" (2 Timothy 1:7, NKJV).

In order to realize God's plan, we must give our life to Him.[3] And the place to start is church.

"Therefore encourage one another and build each other up, just as in fact you are doing" (1 Thessalonians 5:11, NIV).

Father, I am grateful that your mercies are new every morning. Help me to live accordingly, never taking for granted the gift of salvation or the freedom to attend church. I am blessed.

1. 1 Corinthians 13:13
2. Ephesians 5:19
3. Romans 14:8

Your Thoughts . . .

Sunday Thought:
Imposter Syndrome

God knows our hearts even better than we,
So when in self-doubt, pray;
And keep an ear out for his answer,
Never mind what your own mind may say.

HAVE YOU EVER BECOME overwhelmed with self-doubt, insecurity, or a feeling of unworthiness? In professional circles, this state of agitation is known as Impostor Syndrome. Many people experience it; I know I have.

The same thing can happen to us as Christians. Maybe you have a past that you're not proud of, and feel like you're not worthy of forgiveness. Or you might feel like a fraud around your church family, who only know you as a Christian—not the "old you."

Well, first of all, none of us are worthy. That's why we are saved by grace. And when you get saved, the "old you" is dead.[1] So check that off your list.

1. Romans 6:6

"For by grace you have been saved through faith, and that not of yourselves; it is the gift of God, not of works, lest anyone should boast" (Ephesians 2:8–9, NKJV).

If you Google "how to overcome Impostor Syndrome," the first article that pops up lists eight steps to take. Though it is geared toward business professionals, I found it uncanny how relevant these steps are to the Christian walk . . . and sure enough, there is Scriptural backup for each and every one.

1. Know you're not alone:

". . . I will never leave you nor forsake you" (Hebrews 13:5, NKJV).

2. Distinguish humility and fear:

"For God has not given us a spirit of fear . . ." (2 Timothy 1:7, NKJV).

3. Let go of your inner perfectionist:

"Not that we are sufficient of ourselves to think of anything as being from ourselves, but our sufficiency is from God" (2 Corinthians 3:5, NKJV).

4. Be kind to yourself:

". . . Love your neighbor as yourself" (Mark 12:31, NIV).

5. Track and measure your successes:

"Therefore do not cast away your confidence, which has great reward" (Hebrews 10:35, NKJV).

6. Talk about it with a mentor:

"Where there is no counsel, the people fall; But in the multitude of counselors there is safety" (Proverbs 11:14, NKJV).

7. Say yes to new opportunities:

"But we will give ourselves continually to prayer and to the ministry of the word" (Acts 6:4, NKJV).

8. Embrace the feeling and use it:

"A man's pride will bring him low, but the humble in spirit will retain honor" (Proverbs 29:23, NKJV).

If you as a Christian struggle with Imposter Syndrome, I encourage you to study these verses!

"For if our heart condemns us, God is greater than our heart, and knows all things" (1 John 3:20, NKJV).

Dear Lord, help me to remember that you know my heart even better than I do! Bolster me up with your Word; strengthen me to do your work. I know I can do all things through Christ who strengthens me.

SUNDAY THOUGHTS

Your Thoughts . . .

_____

_____

_____

_____

_____

_____

_____

_____

_____

_____

_____

_____

_____

_____

_____

_____

_____

_____

_____

_____

_____

_____

_____

_____

_____

_____

_____

_____

_____

Sunday Thought:
Living in Fear

We should know God with a fearful respect
And give him, in faith, our lives to direct.

"THE FEAR OF THE Lord is the beginning of knowledge, but fools despise wisdom and instruction" (Proverbs 1:7, NKJV).

Many people live their lives in fear—the mortal fear of death. But, while none of us look forward to dying, we are assured in the Bible that we need not fear death! By the grace of God, our spirits can have eternal life after our physical bodies die.

"For God so loved the world that He gave His only begotten Son, that whoever believes in Him should not perish but have everlasting life" (John 3:16, NKJV).

There is another way to live. In the Bible, we are exhorted to fear the Lord. This doesn't mean quaking in our shoes, waiting to be struck down; it means living for

God. Trusting him, loving him, and revering his power and authority in our lives.

"... what does the LORD your God require of you, but to fear the LORD your God, to walk in all His ways and to love Him, to serve the LORD your God with all your heart and with all your soul" (Deuteronomy 10:12, NKJV).

If you're going to live in fear, live in the fear of the Lord.

Oh Lord, help me to live my life in fearful respect of your power. Grant me understanding of your Word and your love, which is more powerful that any other force. Let your love shine through me and be a light to others.

Your Thoughts . . .

_____

_____

_____

_____

_____

_____

_____

_____

_____

_____

_____

_____

_____

_____

_____

Sunday Thought:
Testimony

The years you thought were wasted
Are but chapters in your story;
Will you hide them in regret
Or use them for his glory?

"And they overcame him by the blood of the Lamb, and by the word of their testimony; and they loved not their lives unto the death" (Revelation 12:11, KJV).

We've touched on the topic of testimonies, but let's dive deeper. A person's testimony is the story of their spiritual journey and conversion. We all have different stories: some Christians are raised in the church and never know any other way of life, while others convert later in life— some even on their death beds.

I personally feel like an in-betweener. I was brought up in the church and baptized at the age of nineteen, but fell away for many years. I always felt pulled to go back, and have been a happier person ever since I did! I now recognize how God was working in my life all of those intervening years, even when I wasn't living for him.

During that time, among other things, I endured an abusive marriage; but, while it's always a shame when that happens, it did help shape the person I am today. The truth is, I could have been killed; but I believe that God protected me because he had a higher purpose for me.

You see, what I went through helped build my *testimony*. I've heard some Christians express regret over the "wasted years" before they accepted Christ—but we must remember that those years are chapters in our story. And it is a more profound witness when a person makes a drastic change in their life.

There are many examples in the Bible of the power of testimonies. We need to share our stories with others, and continue to live them each day, even through the hard times. Just remember that it's easy to praise God when life is good; it's when a Christian faithfully endures suffering that people start to pay attention.

"And this is the testimony: that God has given us eternal life, and this life is in His Son" (1 John 5:11, NKJV).

What is your testimony?

Dear God, please help me to live my life as an example for others. If it be your will, use the change I made from the person I used to be as an encouragement to anyone who might feel like their past cannot be overcome. Use my life to your purpose, Lord.

Your Thoughts . . .

_____

_____

_____

_____

_____

_____

_____

_____

_____

_____

_____

_____

_____

_____

_____

_____

_____

_____

_____

_____

_____

_____

_____

_____

_____

_____

_____

_____

_____

_____

_____

Sunday Thought:
Be Still

Caught up in the day to day,
The years will come and go;
Make sure that you are making time
To just be still, and know.

LIFE IS FULL OF distractions. One day I was sitting in a hospital cafeteria with a friend, and there were so many distractions that it was hard even to focus as she prayed over our food. Not only was there the background noise of other people, but a television was turned up *and* music was playing through the speakers. I was reminded in that moment of the verse in Psalms:

"Be still, and know that I am God . . ." (Psalm 46:10, NKJV).

It's too much, people! Too much noise. Too much busyness. Too many distractions from the things that are truly important. I have always enjoyed my quiet time, but even so I too am guilty sometimes of overstimulating my brain, often with audio books and movies. And I have to remind myself to be still, and make time for God. Time for prayer, and getting into the Word. There are many scriptures in which we are exhorted and encouraged to be still; below are just a few of them.

"Be still before the LORD and wait patiently for him . . ." (Psalm 37:7, ESV).

"For God alone, O my soul, wait in silence, for my hope is from him" (Psalm 62:5, ESV).

"Surely I have calmed and quieted my soul . . ." (Psalm 131:2, NKJV).

If you need more stillness in your life, take the time to read your Bible. I try to read regularly; and even though I miss some days, I'm still devoting more time to it than I ever have before. Writing these devotions also gives me quiet time in which to meditate on Scripture.

I also recommend keeping a prayer journal. I started one in the beginning of 2023, and it is very fulfilling! When you are writing something down, your brain has to take time and focus on it. And what do we need in order to focus?

Quiet.

Find a way that works for you. Because when we let ourselves be still and know God, we also find peace.

"You will keep him in perfect peace, whose mind is stayed on You, because he trusts in You" (Isaiah 26:3, NKJV).

Just as our body needs to be still to rest, so does our mind.

"Come unto me, all ye that labour and are heavy laden, and I will give you rest" (Matthew 11:28, KJV).

Thank you, Lord, for the reminder to be still. Help me to continue to grow in faith; to put aside the distractions, read your Word, and get to know you better.

Your Thoughts . . .

_____

_____

_____

_____

_____

_____

_____

_____

_____

_____

_____

_____

_____

_____

_____

_____

_____

_____

_____

_____

Sunday Thought:
A Great Marriage

Just as we take wedding vows,
  We pledge ourselves to him
  When we accept salvation;
  Then the real work begins.

A WEDDING IS THE union of two people by marriage vows, and is often a large celebration. However, those of us who are married understand that it takes a lot of work moving forward to maintain that relationship. Ideally, you learn to better understand one another, and grow closer and more trusting of each other throughout the years.

It is the same concept when we accept Jesus as our Savior. The church is the bride of heaven, and when you accept Christ you become a member of that church.

"For this reason a man shall leave his father and mother and be joined to his wife, and the two shall become one flesh. This is a great mystery, but I speak concerning Christ and the church" (Ephesians 5:31–32, NKJV).

As a bride prepares for her wedding day, so must we make ourselves ready.[2] And, as the wedding is the celebratory beginning of a new relationship, so is the day that each of us attains salvation.

But after that, the real work begins! We need to get to know God, and understand his love and sacrifice. We must fight the good fight,[3] trusting him and studying to show ourselves approved.

"Be diligent to present yourself approved to God, a worker who does not need to be ashamed, rightly dividing the word of truth" (2 Timothy 2:15, NKJV).

Help me, oh Lord, to always strive to continue in learning and growing in faith. Help me to bring glory to your name as a representative of Christ here on the earth.

Your Thoughts . . .

_____

_____

_____

_____

_____

_____

_____

_____

_____

_____

_____

_____

2. Revelation 19:7
3. 1 Timothy 6:12

Sunday Thought:
Maybe Later

How presumptive are we to put God off,
We mortals who don't know the date
That our time here will end,
And for all that we know,
Any later may be too late.

IT HAS BEEN SAID that today is a gift, and that's why it is called the present. But a lot of folks put the pleasures of this world ahead of their relationship with God, thinking, "I'll get baptized later, after I've had my fun," or, "just in case." I know I've been guilty before of putting God on the back burner.

But many wait until it's too late. We never know which day will be our last on this earth, and shouldn't take for granted that we'll have a "later" in which to accept Jesus. I cannot stress enough how the joy of living for Christ supersedes the pleasures of the world.

". . . Behold, now is the accepted time; behold, now is the day of salvation" (2 Corinthians 6:2, NKJV).

We need to make sure our priorities are in order. Surely it is better to suffer worldly persecution than to suffer the words, "I never knew you; depart from Me."[1]

Life on earth is fleeting, but even the concept of eternity is beyond our comprehension. You have an immortal soul—but it's up to you to decide where it will go. Rather than live in dread of death, how much better to rest in the promise: "Assuredly, I say to you, today you will be with Me in Paradise."[2]

Dear God, I pray that you be with my friends and loved ones who don't know you. Help me to lead them to you, and to trust in your timing and your will for their lives. Use me to your purpose, Lord.

Your Thoughts . . .

_____

_____

_____

_____

_____

_____

_____

_____

_____

_____

1. Matthew 7:23
2. Luke 23:43

Sunday Thought:
Faith to Faith

When I'm focused on my troubles
Remind me to step back;
Remind me, Lord, that my reward
Will far outweigh the bad

". . . THE righteousness of God is revealed from faith to faith; as it is written, 'the just shall live by faith'" (Romans 1:17, NKJV).

We like to take pictures of the happy moments in our lives, but there are often difficult times in between. Struggling is never fun; but we get through these moments, growing and learning in the process.

It's the same in our Christian walk. When we trust in God as we endure trials, he reveals himself to us and grows our faith.

"It's as if my tears were my soul's way of watering what God was doing inside of me."
—Gretchen Saffles, *The Well-Watered Woman*

An excellent example of this is Job. Job was a faithful follower of God, who, being tested by the devil, lost in one fell swoop all of his livestock, servants, and even his children. Though he knew grief as well as any other man living,[1] Job remained faithful:

"The Lord gave, and the Lord hath taken away; blessed be the name of the Lord" (Job 1:21, KJV).

Ultimately, God rewarded Job's faithfulness with more than he had ever lost.[2] This should serve as a reminder for us: when we remain faithful, God will reward us, if not on earth then in Heaven.

"Rejoice, and be exceeding glad: for great is your reward in heaven" (Matthew 5:12, KJV).

Your Thoughts . . .

_____

_____

_____

_____

_____

_____

_____

_____

_____

_____

_____

_____

1. Job 16:16
2. Job 42:10

Sunday Thought:
But God

Sarah bore a child, though she was old;
Lazarus rose from the sod;
The fish swallowed Jonah when it was told;
All impossible . . . but God.

FREQUENTLY THROUGHOUT THE BIBLE we find two little words: but God. We see them whenever there is hope amidst despair. Joseph was sold into Egypt—*but God* was with him.[1] Saul sought David to kill him—*but God* kept him safe.[2] *But God* remembered Noah, and all those in the ark.[3]

These words also demonstrate the power of God:

"You killed the author of life, but God raised him from the dead" (Acts 3:15, NIV).

They offer spiritual encouragement to his people:

1. Acts 7:9
2. 1 Samuel 23:14
3. Genesis 8:1

". . . but with God all things are possible" (Matthew 19:26, NKJV).

I was impressed recently when a friend on social media shared a birthday post for her son. She wrote that he was "the baby I wasn't supposed to be able to have . . . but God . . ."

I thought it was a wonderful testimony! Whenever we're struggling, we need to remember: *but God*.

Heavenly Father, help me to remember that anything is possible through you. I thank you for the miracles that you perform every day, and for the testimonies of those who receive them. Open my eyes to your goodness, Lord, that I may always give you the glory.

Your Thoughts . . .

_____

_____

_____

_____

_____

_____

_____

_____

_____

_____

_____

_____

_____

_____

_____

Sunday Thought:
Judge Not

Judge not your enemy, nor your brother;
Correct, and don't condone;
But let he who is without a sin
Be first to cast a stone.

WE ARE ALL GUILTY of judging other people. Sometimes it's hard not to; we're only human. But the Bible reminds us repeatedly that we are no better than anyone else. In fact, we are exhorted to treat others as more important than ourselves.[1]

"Judge not, that ye be not judged" (Matthew 7:1, KJV).

There is a well-known expression among Christians: "There but for the grace of God go I." John Bradford, who coined the expression, was an English evangelical preacher who lived in the 1500s. Bradford was heard to say, as he

1. Philippians 2:3

saw a group of criminals being led to their execution, "But for the grace of God, there goes John Bradford."

We ought to humble ourselves in this way, remembering that only God knows what life we might be leading if not for his grace. This is not to say that those of us under grace won't have troubles or afflictions in this life; indeed, many Christians come from troubled backgrounds. But these are testimonies, which should be shared and used to glorify God. Your story could touch the heart of that homeless person you just passed on the sidewalk!

"But by the grace of God I am what I am . . ." (1 Corinthians 15:10, KJV).

John Bradford was martyred by burning at the stake on July 15th, 1555. He had been in prison for nearly two years; and when the news came of the appointed time, he replied, "I thank God for it . . . the Lord make me worthy thereof."

"Or do you not know that wrongdoers will not inherit the kingdom of God? . . . And that is what some of you were. But you were washed, you were sanctified, you were justified in the name of the Lord Jesus Christ and by the Spirit of our God" (1 Corinthians 6:9,11, NIV).

Thank you, Lord, for saving me from the person I used to be. Remind me not to judge others, but to stay humble and loving, remembering who I once was and still would be, if it weren't for you.

Your Thoughts . . .

_____

_____

_____

_____

_____

_____

_____

_____

_____

_____

_____

_____

_____

_____

_____

_____

_____

_____

_____

_____

_____

_____

_____

_____

_____

_____

Sunday Thought:

Desiring Mercy

We ought to show compassion
As has been shown to us
Showing mercy and forgiving,
Not exacting sacrifice.

IN THE OLD TESTAMENT, God says through the prophet Hosea:

"For I desire mercy and not sacrifice, and the knowledge of God more than burnt offerings" (Hosea 6:6, NKJV).

This is the first of three times that we read this statement in the Bible; but what does it mean? In the gospel of Matthew, Jesus exhorts us to learn:

"'. . . Those who are well have no need of a physician, but those who are sick. But go and learn what this means: 'I desire mercy and not sacrifice.' For I did not come to call the righteous, but sinners, to repentance'" (Matthew 9:12, 13, NKJV).

In this situation, Jesus is standing up for the guilty. A few chapters later, we find him using the same expression to stand up for the innocent:

"'But if you had known what this means, 'I desire mercy and not sacrifice,' you would not have condemned the guiltless'" (Matthew 12:7, NKJV).

Clearly, it is the desire of God to show mercy on us. It's what he *wants*. And we are to follow his example.

"'. . . and to love your neighbor as yourself is more important than all burnt offerings and sacrifices'" (Mark 12:33, NIV).

God does not want us to live our lives carrying the burden of past sins. Nor does he want us to offer sacrifices or other works in atonement for our sins. We must remember that we are under grace, not law,[1] and that no work can ever *earn* salvation.[2]

God wants us to come to him; to accept him into our lives, and be forgiven by his grace, through our faith.

"For by grace you have been saved through faith, and that not of yourselves; it is the gift of God, not of works, lest anyone should boast" (Ephesians 2:8–9, NKJV).

"Mercy is of God, and therefore has no end."
—Ray Ortlund, "Mercy Not Sacrifice"

1. Galatians 5:18
2. Romans 11:6

Dear God, I thank you for your mercy and grace, through which I am saved. Help me to be forgiving of others, as you have been to me.

Your Thoughts . . .

_____

_____

_____

_____

_____

_____

_____

_____

_____

_____

_____

_____

_____

_____

_____

_____

_____

_____

_____

_____

_____

_____

_____

_____

_____

_____

Sunday Thought:
Vengeance is Mine

Do not repay evil for evil,
But meet with forgiveness the sword
Bless your very enemies-
For vengeance is mine, says the Lord.

WE'VE ALL HEARD THE expression "turn the other cheek," and as Christians, have likely been advised at some point to do so. While this is certainly scriptural advice,[1] it can be extremely difficult to do. So this week I want to offer further encouragement on this topic.

The Bible talks quite a lot about how to handle tough situations. First of all, we need to understand that we are not simply told to bear up and never pay any mind to the things people say or do. God sees and knows all, including when his people are being persecuted. We are told to turn the other cheek because he will handle it![2]

1. Matthew 5:39
2. 2 Thessalonians 1 6–7

We are instructed to bless those who persecute us,[3] and even to repay our enemy with kindness.[4]

". . . For in so doing you will heap coals of fire on his head" (Romans 12:20, NKJV).

These instructions can be pretty discouraging, if taken out of context. I have prayed for people who are difficult for me to pray for—so difficult at times that I have had to rely on the Holy Spirit to intercede for me, as we are promised he will do.[5]

"But I say to you, love your enemies, bless those who curse you, do good to those who hate you, and pray for those who spitefully use you and persecute you" (Matthew 5:44, NKJV).

If Jesus could pray for the men who were crucifying him on the cross, surely we can pray for those who persecute us. Perhaps we ought even to pray the same prayer, and ask God to forgive them—for they know not what they do. Because surely no evil deed is worth spending eternity in the lake of fire.

It is our job as Christians to give these cares to God, and pray that our enemies seek his mercy. And for those who refuse, well . . .

"'Vengeance is mine, I will repay,' says the Lord" (Romans 12:19, NKJV).

3. Romans 12:14
4. Romans 12:20
5. Romans 8:26

Oh God, it is hard to turn the other cheek! Help me to trust that you are with me when I endure persecution; that you understand, and will give me the strength to persevere. Help me to be forgiving of those who wrong me, and to leave them in your hands.

Your Thoughts . . .

_____

_____

_____

_____

_____

_____

_____

_____

_____

_____

_____

_____

_____

_____

_____

_____

_____

_____

_____

_____

_____

_____

_____

_____

Sunday Thought:
Handsome Devil

Beware the fallen angel,
Resist the father of lies
Put on the armor of God and know
The devil in his guise.

CONTRARY TO POPULAR MEDIA depictions, the devil doesn't always look like a scary ghoul, or a little red man with a pointed tail. In fact, we are warned in the Bible that Satan often makes his presence known in ways that appeal to us, rather than those that would repel us. It makes sense, as this is a far more effective tactic; and, after all, he is a fallen angel.[1]

". . . For Satan himself transforms himself into an angel of light" (2 Corinthians 11:14, NKJV).

1. Revelation 12:9

There are many and varied ways in which the devil will try to get at us as a society. He may appear as a false prophet,[2] or he may influence those in power: world leaders, or those who write legislature that clothe in eloquent words an act against God.

"Be sober, be vigilant; because your adversary the devil walks about like a roaring lion, seeking whom he may devour" (1 Peter 5:8, NKJV).

And he will certainly attack us individually. Whether it be through physical temptation, pride, gluttony, idolatry, or some other medium, he will use whatever means he thinks we are most susceptible to.

Watch out for that handsome devil.

"I don't believe Old Nick can be so very ugly. He wouldn't do so much harm if he was. I always think of him as a rather handsome gentleman."

—L.M. Montgomery, *Anne of the Island*

Dear God, please open my eyes that I may recognize the devil when I see him. Help me to always be on my guard against his many forms, and give me strength when he would prey on my weakness. Guide me in study as I arm myself with your Word.

2. Ezekiel 13:9

SUNDAY THOUGHTS

Your Thoughts . . .

_____

_____

_____

_____

_____

_____

_____

_____

_____

_____

_____

_____

_____

_____

_____

_____

_____

_____

_____

_____

_____

_____

_____

_____

_____

_____

_____

_____

Sunday Thought:
Thank God

In life and in prayer, let us imbue
A humble spirit of gratitude.

How many times in your life have you felt relieved and said, "Thank God!" Well, chances are you don't know how right you were. We ought not to say it lightly, but should with genuine gratitude and humility acknowledge our Father in all things.[1]

Our society does focus on being thankful and generous during the holidays—and this is a good thing. But we should be thanking God and counting our blessings all the time, not just once a year.

For Christians, this so-called "holiday spirit" is actually the Holy Spirit; and yes, we feel it year round. If you are looking for that joy and peace in your own life, start by reading the Gospel.[2] Learn and understand what Jesus has done for you. Invite God into your life, and go to church

1. Colossians 3:17
2. 1 Corinthians 15:3–4

to keep learning and being encouraged. Understand God's grace—and always be thankful for it.

". . . let us continually offer the sacrifice of praise to God, that is, the fruit of our lips, giving thanks to His name" (Hebrews 13:15, NKJV).

Thank you, Father, for all of my blessings. For your Son, whose sacrifice paid for my salvation, and for your Spirit, who fills me with joy. Help me to live accordingly, that those around me might see you shining through.

Your Thoughts . . .

_____

_____

_____

_____

_____

_____

_____

_____

_____

_____

_____

_____

_____

_____

_____

_____

_____

_____

_____

Sunday Thought:
Good News!

We live not in fear of death,
But in anticipation
Thanks to Jesus' sacrifice
And gift of salvation.

WHAT IS THE GOOD News that Christians are always talking about? Let's start in the book of Luke, on the day of Jesus' birth:

"And the angel said to them, 'Fear not, for behold, I bring you good news of great joy that will be for all the people. For unto you is born this day in the city of David a Savior, who is Christ the Lord'" (Luke 2:10–11, ESV).

The Good News is the Gospel of Jesus Christ: the foundation and basic theology of the Christian religion. It is summarized in one of Paul's letters to the Corinthians:

"Moreover, brethren, I declare to you the gospel which I preached to you, which also you received and in which you stand, by which also

you are saved, if you hold fast that word which
I preached to you—unless you believed in vain.
"For I delivered to you first of all that
which I also received: that Christ died for our
sins according to the Scriptures, and that He
was buried, and that He rose again the third
day according to the Scriptures" (1 Corinthians
15:1–4, NKJV).

The Good News is the gift of salvation—and it's a
gift that keeps on giving! Living for God gives us a higher
purpose, peace of mind, and a joyful heart. A new heart,
in fact:

"I will give you a new heart and put a new spirit
within you; I will take the heart of stone out of your flesh
and give you a heart of flesh" (Ezekiel 36:26, NKJV).

So what are you waiting for? If you don't have this
peace and joy in your life, you can have it today. Jesus is
waiting with open arms; and you'll find that once you've
experienced God's love and mercy, you too will want to
share the Good News!

"... Go ye into all the world, and preach the gospel to
every creature" (Mark 16:15, KJV).

*Heavenly Father, I thank you for your gift of salvation.
Help me to illustrate your Good News by the way I live my
life. Give me the wisdom to know what to say to whom, and
when not to speak. Let my actions reflect your love.*

Your Thoughts . . .

_____

_____

_____

_____

_____

_____

_____

_____

_____

_____

_____

_____

_____

_____

_____

_____

_____

_____

_____

_____

_____

_____

_____

_____

_____

_____

_____

_____

_____

Sunday Thought:

Amen

God above is first and last,
The beginning and the end;
In show of our agreement,
Let His people say "Amen."

IN CHURCH WE OFTEN hear people say "amen," either during the preacher's sermon, or perhaps after a testimony has been given. This is a positive affirmation, showing a person's agreement with what is being said.

"... And so through him the "Amen" is spoken by us to the glory of God" (2 Corinthians 1:20, NIV).

The original Hebrew word "amen" translates to "verily," or "truly;" and it is generally written this way in English versions of Scripture. For example, when Jesus speaks:

"Verily, verily, I say unto you, He that believeth on me, the works that I do shall he do also . . ." (John 14:12, KJV).

It is interesting to note that in verses like these, Jesus is using the expression at the beginning of his sentence, rather than at the end. To me, this conveys the importance of what is being said; like Jesus is saying, "Hear what I say, and believe that it is true."

Then there are verses that say it twice at the end of a sentence. I believe we should give extra consideration to this emphasis:

"And blessed be His glorious name forever! And let the whole earth be filled with His glory. Amen and Amen" (Psalm 72:19, NKJV).

Finally, the most common way that we hear and say "amen" is at the closing of prayer. In this context it means, "let it be so."

"Blessed be the LORD God of Israel from everlasting to everlasting: and let all the people say, Amen. Praise ye the LORD" (Psalm 106:48, KJV).

Heavenly Father, as this year of devotions comes to a close, I ask that you strengthen my resolve to study your Word. Help me to maintain an attitude of prayer, that I might always turn to you, with both my heavy burdens and daily concerns. Bolster me up with your Word as I arm myself against the devil.

Strengthen me, Lord, as I strive to set a Christ-like example for those around me. Help me to forgive others, as you have forgiven me. Sustain me through life's trials and losses, and encourage me through your Word to trust and obey. Work your will into my life, Lord. I ask these things in Jesus' name. Amen.

SUNDAY THOUGHTS

Your Thoughts . . .

_____
_____
_____
_____
_____
_____
_____
_____
_____
_____
_____
_____
_____
_____
_____
_____
_____
_____
_____
_____
_____
_____
_____
_____
_____
_____
_____
_____

"The fear of the Lord is the beginning of knowledge, but fools despise wisdom and instruction" (Proverbs 1:7, NKJV).

www.ingramcontent.com/pod-product-compliance
Lightning Source LLC
Chambersburg PA
CBHW052011090426
42741CB00008B/1650